AF413246

Our Kitchen

Executive Chef Mohamad N. Hachem

Illustrator:Sofia Ktivets
Editor: Zeinab Zaiter Hachem

ISBN: 979-8-3304-1369-0

Lentil Soup

Ingredients:

- 1 cup red split lentils
- 3 cups of cold water
- 1 onion
- 1 carrot
- 1 potato
- 1 lemon
- ½ tbsp salt approx
- 1 tsp of vegetable broth (optional)

Instructions:

Wash the lentils in a fine strainer by running them under cold water.
Add the lentils to a medium pot with cold water and bring to boil on medium high heat.
Remove most of the white foam that rises to the surface with a spoon and discard.
Roughly chop the carrot, onion, potato and add them to the lentils along with the salt.
Cook for another 20 or so minutes until the potato is done.
Turn off the heat and blitz with a hand blender.
Taste test and adjust the salt.
Serve in a bowl and add squeezed lemons per choice.

Lentil with Chard soup

 Prep Time: 5 mins    Cook Time: 25 mins    Serves: 8 Servings

Ingredients:

- 1 cup lentils
- 8 cups of cold water
- 1 ½ cups swiss chard
- ¼ tsp seven spice
- ½ tsp sumac

- 2 tsp salt
- 2 medium potatoes
- 1 large onion
- 2 garlic cloves
- 1 cup coriander (cilantro)
- 1 lemon juiced

Instructions:

Add the lentils to cold water and bring to boil. Then cook the lentils for about 15 minutes over medium heat.

Peel the potatoes, cut them into cubes, and add potatoes to the pot. Roughly chop the chard and add it to the pot.

Add seven spices, sumac, salt, and cook for another 15 minutes until the potatoes are well done.

In a pan, sauté the onions in some mild olive oil until golden, then add the garlic and coriander, and sauté for a few more minutes.

Then add this mixture to the lentils and stir.

Add the lemon just before you turn off the heat and adjust the seasoning and water levels with some boiling water if necessary.

Drizzle with a small amount of extra virgin olive oil before serving.

Chicken Mushroom soup

 Prep Time: 20 mins　 Cook Time: 1 hour　 Serves: 5 Servings

Ingredients:

- 3 pulled chicken breast
- 2 minced garlic cloves
- 1 tbsp minced ginger
- 3 cups milk
- 2 cups water
- 1 cup liquid whipping cream

- 2 packs fresh mushroom
- 2 tbsp soft butter
- 1 tsp black pepper
- 1 tsp salt
- 1 tsp dried ground thyme
- 1 tsp oregano

Instructions:

Cut the chicken breast into small cubes.
Slice the mushrooms.
In a pan, melt butter and roast the chicken until golden. Add salt, black pepper, and oregano, then stir well.
Add the mushroom slices and continue stirring until they are cooked.
In a bowl, mix the milk, cream, water, and thyme.
Pour mixture over the chicken and mushrooms, stirring continuously until the mixture thickens to your desired consistency.
Serve the soup in bowls once it reaches the desired texture.

Chicken Soup

 Prep Time: 10 mins    Cook Time: 15 mins    Serves: 4 Servings

Ingredients:

- 4 cups of water
- 1 chicken
- 2 tbsp vegetable oil
- ½ cup of vermicelli
- ½ a lemon

Instructions:

Boil the chicken in water, then remove the chicken and leave the chicken stock on low heat.
Shred your chicken pieces and add to the chicken stock.
In a separate pot, add vegetable oil and the vermicelli.
Keep stirring around on medium heat until the vermicelli becomes heavier to the touch and light golden in color.
Pour in the chicken stock and shredded chicken onto the vermicelli.
Keep simmering for another 10 minutes until the vermicelli is cooked.
Turn off the heat and add the lemon.

Tabouli Salad

 Prep Time: 10 mins  Cook Time: 15 mins  Serves: 5 Servings

Ingredients:

- 1 large parsley
- 2 medium tomatoes
- ⅓ small onion
- 1 stalk spring onion
- 1 large lemon

- sprinkle of salt to taste
- ½ tsp sumac
- 1 tbsp fine bulgur wheat
- extra virgin olive oil

Instructions:

Wash all the ingredients thoroughly.
Finely chop parsley, add to a large bowl.
Slice the tomato into several rings, then finely chop each one.
Chop the mint, onion and spring onion finely.
Sprinkle on sumac and salt.
Soak the bulgur wheat for five minutes before serving.
Add a generous drizzling of extra virgin olive oil, along with the bulgur wheat and lemon juice.
Taste and balance the dressing with extra salt/lemon if required.
Serve with optional lettuce leaves.

Moujadara

 Prep Time: 10 mins    Cook Time: 50 mins    Serves: 6 Servings

Ingredients:

- 4 large onions
- ½ cup regular olive oil
- 1 cups brown lentils
- 1 cup coarse bulgur wheat

- 2 tsp salt
- boiled water
- 3 ½ cups cold water
- extra virgin olive oil

Instructions:

Chop the onions and add them to a pan with olive oil, sprinkle with a little salt.

Sauté on medium heat for at least 20 minutes until they turn dark brown (but not burnt!) The more you brown them the more savory the flavor. Stand back and slowly add enough boiled water to just cover the onions (it will splutter!) and squish them down with the back of a wooden spoon.

Add the salt and bring to boil, cover and simmer on low heat for 10 minutes.

Add the lentils and the cold water, bring to boil then reduce the heat to low and leave to cook for around another half hour until the lentils are cooked

Add the bulgur wheat and simmer for another 15 minutes..

When the bulgur wheat has soaked up most of the liquid, taste and adjust the salt as necessary, turn off the heat and add a dash of olive oil. Serve with a side salad or a helping of plain yoghurt.

Potato Stew

 Prep Time: 10 mins  Cook Time: 30 mins  Serves: 5 Servings

Ingredients:

- 1 large onion
- 2 garlic cloves
- small handful cilantro
- 4 medium potatoes
- ½ pound meat lamb or beef fillet
- 3 tbsp tomato concentrate

- 3 cups of boiling water
- ¼ tsp seven spice
- ¼ tsp black pepper
- ½ tsp salt
- ½ lemon juice

Instructions:

In a casserole dish, add a good drizzle of mild olive oil (2-3 tbsp) and sauté the chopped onion until golden. Then add the cilantro and garlic and sauté for a few more minutes to form the stew base.
Add the chopped lamb or beef fillet and sauté for a few more minutes on medium heat. You can fry the lamb off in a separate pan to avoid a fatty taste.
Chop the potatoes into bite sized chunks.
Add onions and meat and gently sauté for a few minutes, drizzle olive oil.
Add the tomato puree, 7 spice, black pepper, salt and enough boiling water to cover.

Bring to a boil then lower the heat to a simmer for around 20 minutes until the potatoes are well cooked. You can also add an optional drizzle of pomegranate molasses.
Taste and adjust the seasoning before you turn off the heat.
Squeeze on a little lemon when serving according to taste.
Serve with a side salad or a helping of plain yoghurt

Kafta Batata

 Prep Time: 10 mins    Cook Time: 40 mins    Serves: 6 Servings

Ingredients:

For the meatballs
- 1.5 pounds of ground beef
- 1 onion
- 1 cup parsley
- ¼ tsp black pepper
- 1 tsp seven spice
- ¼ tsp salt

- 3 medium potatoes
- vegetable oil
- 2 onions
- 3 tbsp olive oil
- 3 cups boiling water
- 4 tomatoes
- 2 tbsp tomato juice
- ½ tbsp salt

Instructions:

Meatballs:
In a food processor, finely chop the onion and parsley.
In a mixing bowl, add the ground beef, spices and salt along with the parsley and onions.
Knead together well until evenly distributed. You can also combine everything in the food processor until you have a fine texture.
Shape into small balls.
Kafta:
Cut the potatoes into bite sized chunks, then deep fry half way until slightly golden, set aside.

Cut the onions in half, then into strips. Sauté in a pot with a good drizzle of regular olive oil until golden.
Add the tomato juice, chopped fresh tomatoes and 3 cups of boiling water along with the salt.
Bring to boil then add the potatoes and reduce to medium heat.
After 20 minutes when the potatoes are done, add the meatballs and simmer for another ten minutes.
Add the tomato puree, 7 spice, black pepper, salt and enough boiling water to cover. Bring to a boil then lower the heat to a simmer for around 20 minutes until the potatoes are well cooked.

Vegetarian Stuffed Grape Leaves

 Prep Time: 2 hours    Cook Time: 1 hours    Serves: 10 Servings

Ingredients:

- 1 Jar of grape leaves or 50-70 fresh leaves
- 2 medium potatoes
- 2 large bunches of parsley
- 8 medium tomatoes
- 2-3 spring onions
- ⅓ of a medium onion
- 2 cups of short grain rice
- 2 lemons juiced
- 1 tbsp tomato juice
- 1 tbsp salt
- 1 tbsp seven spice
- ½ cup of regular olive oil
- 1 cup of water

Instructions:

If you are using fresh leaves, blanche them in hot water for five minutes and drain. If you are using grape leaves from the jar, rinse them in cold water and drain
Finely chop the parsley, tomatoes and onions. Add to a bowl.
Add the rice, salt, 7 spice, tomato juice, olive oil and the juice of 1 lemon to the bowl and stir well.
Peel the potatoes and slice approximately 1 cm thick and arrange them at the bottom of the pot.
Prepare your work area with one tray to roll the grape leaves beside the mixture and cooking pot.
Lay out one grape leaf on the tray and remove any stems.
Add 1 tablespoon of mixture in the middle of the grape leaf and tuck in the sides. Roll up firmly into a cigar shape.
Stack the grape leaves into layers in the pot.
When you finish rolling the grape leaves, add ½ teaspoon of salt to 1 cup of water and the juice of half a lemon to make the brine.
Press down the grape leaves with a sturdy plate or lid one size smaller than your pot. Pour on enough brine to cover and turn the heat on to medium high.
After 20 minutes, reduce the heat to low and remove the plate/lid. Taste the brine that has come to the surface and adjust the salt/lemon levels as necessary. Cook for another hour on the lowest heat setting.
Taste one stuffed grape leaf before you turn the heat off to make sure the leaves are well done.

Meat Stuffed Grape Leaves

 Prep Time: 1 hours    Cook Time: 1 hours    Serves: 10 Servings

Ingredients:

- 2 jars of grape leaves or 50-70 fresh grape leaves

For the stuffing
- ½ pound of minced lamb or beef
- 1 small onion
- 2 tomatoes
- ¼ tsp black pepper
- ¼ tsp white pepper

- ⅛ tsp turmeric
- ¾ tsp seven spice
- 1 tsp salt
- small handful of parsley
- ¼ cup regular olive oil
- 11/2 cup short grain rice

For the tomato sauce
- 2 cups of tomato juice
- 2 lemons juiced

- ¾ tbsp salt
- 2 tbsp of regular olive oil
- 2-3 garlic cloves

Instructions:

To prepare the grape leaves:
If you are using fresh leaves, trim the stalks and soak them in boiling hot water for five minutes and drain. If you are using grape leaves from the jar, rinse them in cold water and drain. To prepare the stuffing: Wash the rice and soak in some water for around half an hour. Then drain the rice and add to a large mixing bowl.

Add the mince meat, chopped tomatoes, parsley, onion, seven spice,
white and black pepper, salt and oil. Mix well and set aside.
To make the grape leaves:
Lay out one grape leaf on the plate and add 1 tablespoon of stuffing in
the middle of the grape leaf and tuck in the sides. Roll up firmly and
gently into a cigar shape.
Adjust the stuffing amount depending on the size of the leaf.
Stack the rolled up grape leaves on the large tray.
When you have rolled up a good batch, take five or six pieces and
place in a circle rotation position.
When you have finished stacking all the grape leaves, add tomato sauce
on top of them, salt, regular olive oil, juice of 1 lemon and top up
with water if necessary.
Bring to boil then reduce the heat to a low simmer.
After half an hour of cooking, add the garlic and juice of another lemon.
Cover the pot with a lid.
Simmer for another half an hour and taste the sauce to see if it needs
any seasoning, salt or lemon adjustment.
Taste one grape leaf to ensure it is done before turning off the heat.
The total cooking time should be around one hour.

Stuffed Zucchini

 Prep Time: 30 mins  Cook Time: 1 hours  Serves: 8 Servings

Ingredients:

- 5 pounds of green zucchini

For the stuffing
- 1 pound of ground beef
- 1 small onion
- 2 tomatoes
- ¼ tsp black pepper
- ¼ tsp white pepper
- ⅛ tsp turmeric
- ¾ tsp seven spice
- 1 tsp salt
- small handful of parsley
- 10-15 mint leaves
- ¼ cup regular olive oil
- 11/2 cup short grain rice

Our Kitchen

For the tomato sauce
- 3 cups of tomato juice
- 2 lemons juiced
- ¾ tablespoon salt
- 2 tablespoon of regular olive oil
- 2-3 garlic cloves roughly chopped

Instructions:

To prepare the zucchini:
Wash the zucchini well. Remove the tops and set aside if you are going to close the zucchini with them. Using an apple corer, scrape out the insides of the zucchini leaving around a half centimeter.
To prepare the stuffing:
Wash the rice and soak in some water for around half an hour. Then drain the rice and add to a large mixing bowl. Add the group meat, chopped tomatoes, parsley, mint, onion, seven spice, white and black pepper, salt and oil. Mix well and set aside.
To make the stuffed zucchini:
Prepare a large pot to stack the zucchini in.
Take small handful of the stuffing and gently fill the zucchini leaving around an inch near the top for the cooked rice to expand.
Stuff the ends either with the original zucchini. Stack the zucchini in the large pot.
Once you have finished stuffing all the zucchini, add the tomato juice, salt, regular olive oil, juice of 1 lemon and top up with water.
Cover with a plate that fits inside the pot and bring to boil.
Then reduce the heat to a low simmer.
After half an hour of cooking, remove the plate and add the garlic, and juice of another lemon.
Simmer for another half an hour and taste the sauce to see if it needs any seasoning, salt or lemon adjustment.

Fried Kibbe

 Prep Time: 1 hours    Cook Time: 20 mins    Serves: 40 Servings

Ingredients:

For the Kibbe filling
- 2 pounds ground beef
- 2-3 onions
- 1 tsp 7 spice
- 1.5 tbsp kamouneh Kibbeh Spices

- ½ tsp black pepper
- 1 tbsp salt
- 1 cup pine nuts
- 2 tbsp sumac

For the Kibbeh casing
- 2 pounds fine bulgur wheat (#1)
- 2 pounds ground beef
- 2 onions
- 1.5 tbsp Kibbeh Spices

- 1.5 tbsp corn flour
- 1 tsp seven spice
- ½ tsp black pepper
- 1 tbsp salt
- sunflower or vegetable oil

Instructions:

Soak the bulgur wheat in enough water to cover and set aside.
To make the filling, sauté the chopped onions in regular olive oil
until golden on medium low heat.
Add ground beef to the onions and cook out the meat on medium
high heat. Add the seven spice, kamouneh spices, black pepper and
salt and mix well.
When it is cooked turn off the heat and add the sumac and chopped
pine nuts.
Drain the bulgur wheat and add to a large bowl. Add second 2 pounds
of meat to prepare food processor.
In several batches, add the bulgur wheat and equal amounts of meat to
the food processor and process until it clumps together and starts to roll
in the processor bowl.
Roughly chop 2 onions to go in the food processor along with the
seven spices, kamouneh spices, black pepper and salt.
When you have combined all the meat and bulgur wheat in a bowl, add
the onion spice mix and the corn flour, then bring everything together.
If it is too dry add a bit of water, you don't want it too loose, sticky or
crumbly but so it holds together nicely.
Add half a cup of sunflower oil to a small bowl which you can dip your
fingers into when shaping the kibbeh to avoid sticking.
Take some casing and roll into golf ball size, indent the middle then
hollow out the inside with your index finger turning as you do so until
you have a half shell. Add a spoon of filling and close up the casing.
Compress well with your hands and shape into an oval shape.
Line up the kibbeh on the tray until you finish the filling
Deep fry your kibbeh morsels in sunflower or vegetable oil.

Green beans in oil

 Prep Time: 30 mins    Cook Time: 30 mins    Serves: 9 Servings

Ingredients:

- two pounds green beans
- 2 yellow onions
- 4 pieces of garlic
- 4 large tomatos

- 2 tbsp of olive oil
- 1 cup of tomato sauce
- sprinkle of salt
- 2 cups of water

Instructions:

Break green bean into three pieces and continue until all beans are pieced.
Soak green beans in water for 20 minutes.
In a pot, drizzle olive oil and put in onions that are diced into small cubes while stirring.
Add in garlic and continue to stir.
Add in the green beans.
Add in tomato's that have been cut into small cubes. Continue to stir.
Sprinkle salt and add in the water.
Leave on stove for 30 minutes.
You will know when its done when the saucy water becomes the texture of soft salsa.
Enjoy it hot or cold.

Okra stew in oil with Beef

 Prep Time: 30 mins    Cook Time: 90 mins    Serves: 9 Servings

Ingredients:

- 9 tbsp of vegetable oil
- 2 lbs beef stew meat
- 2 onions,
- 2 garlic cloves
- 1 tsp ground cumin
- 1 tsp ground coriander (4 whole pods)
- cup chopped tomato (peeled)

- 3 tbs tomato paste
- 1 cup stock (beef)
- 2 cups water
- 1 ts salt
- 1 tspblack pepper
- 1 1/2lbs okra
(baby, fresh or frozen)
- 1 lemon

Instructions:

Heat oil in a large stock pot over medium high heat. Working in small batches, brown meat, turning constantly, until browned on all sides, about 10 minutes.

Add onions to meat and saute until translucent, 8-10 minutes.

Add garlic, cumin, coriander, tomatoes, tomato paste, and stock. Stir well. Add salt and pepper to taste.

Cover tightly and cook for about 45 minutes- 1 hour or until meat is tender. Add more water if dry.

Prepare okra by rinsing in cool water. Cut the stem end off each and poke holes in them to absorb the liquid.

Once meat is tender add okra and 1-2 cups water. Pour lemon juice over mixture (this reduces the slimy texture of the okra).
Cook an additional 30-45 minutes on low heat until it has a thick stew consistency and okra is soft.
Serve warm with rice

Cheese Rolls

 Prep Time: 25 mins  Cook Time: 5 mins  Serves: 12 Servings

Ingredients:

- 12 spring roll wrappers
(or 6 sheets of phyllo dough)
- ½ cup akawi
- ½ cup mozzarella cheese
- 2 tb parsley
- ¼ tsp black pepper
- 1 tsp all-purpose flour
- 1 tsp water
- vegetable oil for frying

Our Kitchen

Instructions:

Shred the akawi cheese and place in a medium bowl. Add the chopped parsley and black pepper and mix well.
Place a large plate set aside.
Mix the teaspoon of flour with a little bit of water to make a paste to use as your glue to close the roll.
Cut the phyllo dough in half and turn it so a pointy side is facing you. Spread 1 tablespoon of the cheese filling on top. Fold sides in first, then the bottom over.
Using your fingers or a pastry brush, dab a little of the 'glue' on the triangle bottom and fold the rest of the roll. Repeat until you run out of filling.

Transfer the cheese roll onto the plate seam side down.
Heat up the oil to 350F degrees and drop about 4-5 cheese rolls
at a time. Fry until golden, about 3 minutes. Drain on a paper towel
lined plate.
Drain on a paper towel lined plate. Serve hot.